TRIED
& TRUE

A Primer on Sound Pedagogy

by

Daniel B. Coupland

HILLSDALE
COLLEGE PRESS

**K·12
BOOKS**

Hillsdale College Press
33 East College Street
Hillsdale, Michigan 49242
www.hillsdale.edu

Printed in the United States of America

Printed and bound by Cushing-Malloy, Ann Arbor, Michigan
Cover design by Shanna Cote

TRIED & TRUE: A Primer on Sound Pedagogy

Library of Congress Control Number: 2022906635
ISBN: 978-1-941946-02-2

First printing 2022

Dedicated to My Mentors:
Nerenz, Nork, Labaree, Campbell, Baldwin, and Fennell

Contents

Appendices

Ten Books on Teaching that Every Teacher Should Read

Ten Effective Teaching Techniques that Every Teacher Should
Use in the Classroom

Ten Common Classroom Tasks that Most Likely Require a
Procedure Because They Will Save You Time and
Help You to Avoid Chaos

Preface

My first year of teaching was tough.

The ink on my college diploma was barely dry when I was hired to teach Spanish at a public school just north of Detroit. I had recently completed a number of teacher education courses—including a semester of student teaching—that were supposed to make me "classroom ready" on the first day of school. But even with all of those courses behind me, I was still unprepared for the realities of the classroom. In the first few months of the school year, I struggled just to make it to the 3:30 bell at the end of each school day. Then I would often spend four to six hours in the evening preparing for the next day's classes. Week-after-week this exhausting cycle repeated itself with the weekends offering only a partial respite. I was frustrated, but worse—I felt ineffective. I wondered if the time and energy that I had poured into my work were making any noticeable difference in the lives of my students.

On those days when my frustration boiled over, I would exit my classroom soon after the final bell, turn left, walk down the hallway about 30 yards, turn left *again* into the French teacher's classroom, and collapse into a desk at the back of room. After a few moments of silence, Mademoi-selle Nork, who had been teaching for only six years, would graciously push aside her work, look me straight in the eyes, and ask,

"Ok, what happened?"

"It was awful!" I would confess, staring wide-eyed at the chalkboard on the front wall of her classroom.

"Oh, it couldn't have been *that* bad," she would reply. "Tell me about it."

For the next ten minutes or so, I would describe that day's struggles to Mlle. Nork as best as my weary mind could recall them. She would sit there with hands folded on her desk and listen patiently to my troubles. When I had finished, she would pause momentarily to think and then calmly offer me some advice on how to deal with the pedagogical problems that plagued my teaching.

Some of her suggestions were spot-on, and they helped me to overcome seemingly insurmountable obstacles in my teaching. Other suggestions that she offered required some modification so that they would work in my classroom, with my students, and with my personality. And still others did not and would not work no matter how hard I tried. What helped me to survive my first year of teaching was Mlle. Nork's will-ingness to hear me out, to take my concerns seriously, and to offer me what advice she could. And these conversations—sprinkled across my first few years in the classroom—proba-bly saved my teaching career.

Tried and True

These conversations occurred more than a quarter of a century ago. I am now approaching the end of my third decade in the field of education—first as a high school teacher and now as a teacher of teachers. Over these years, I have taught, trained, observed, evaluated, and mentored hundreds of K-12 educators, many of whom were at the start of their teaching careers. During this time, I have been able to see which pedagogical practices are most effective in the classroom, and I have developed some practical advice for new educators that allows them to start their first years of teaching well and to continue to be successful classroom teachers. Some of the advice in this little book I heard years ago from Mlle. Nork, while most of it I have acquired from decades of watching teachers do their incredibly difficult and complex work in classrooms.

This is not to suggest that the principles in this small text are based solely upon my own experience. As a college professor, I value and support high-quality research on teaching and learning. I am the first to admit that something as complex as teaching needs more research, not less. And those of us who teach teachers should be informed by what quality research can teach us about this work. But if teaching is such a complex human act, then we should be willing to accept and learn from other ways of understanding it, too—including history, philosophy, literature, common sense, and yes, personal experience. The practical advice in this book is informed by all of these ways of knowing. The methods have been tried; they have been proven true.

A Primer

This book is a primer, a brief introductory text on a particular subject. *Primer* (pronounced with a "short" i and rhymes with *trimmer*) should not be confused with its homonym *primer* (pronounced with a "long" i and rhymes with *timer*), a word most often associated with paint or ammunition. Both words come from the Latin word *primarius*, which means primary or first. Perhaps the most well-known book of this type in American history was *The New England Primer* (ca. 1690), a popular schoolbook that included moral lessons, quotations from the Bible, and woodcut illustrations. Some of America's founding fathers used *The New England Primer* to teach their own children how to read.

Many of us still use these kinds of introductory texts even if the word *primer* doesn't appear anywhere in the book. *The Elements of Style*, perhaps the most well-known book on composition in the English language, is a primer. Most readers affectionately refer to this short text (barely over 100 pages) as "Strunk and White" after the authors' surnames, William Strunk, Jr., and E. B. White. In his introduction to the third edition, White all but admits that *The Elements of Style* is a primer when he says that the book "does not pretend to survey the whole field. Rather it proposes to give in brief space the principal requirements of plain English style. It concentrates on fundamentals: the rules of usage and principles of composition most commonly violated" (xiv). By focusing exclusively on the "fundamentals," *The Elements of Style* clearly does not address many important aspects of composition. But the authors do this intentionally. The book is not meant to be comprehensive. Rather "Strunk and White" is designed to be an introductory text—i.e., a primer. The authors simply want to give readers a sound introduction to good writing and nothing more.

I hope that my own writing shows an appreciation for and an application of the principles that *The Elements of Style* has taught to generations of readers and writers. But more than that, I hope to imitate (in a sincere form of flattery) Strunk and White in *how* they communicate their ideas. As a "brief introductory text," *Tried & True* is a humble attempt to do for pedagogy what *The Elements of Style* has done for composition.

Sound Pedagogy

Teaching is an incredibly complex task. Anyone who tells you otherwise has most likely never taught—or, perhaps, has never taught *well*. Good teaching depends on many factors, some of which are beyond the teacher's control. It depends upon what is being taught and to whom. It also depends on the time of day, the day of the week, the week of the month, and the month of the year. Good teaching depends on the lighting, the temperature, the arrangement of the room, and hundreds of other factors. With so many variables, it is amazing that anyone can teach anything to anyone else. Yet teaching *does* occur. Every day, millions of teachers around the globe help millions of learners to know or do something new.

But why focus only on good teaching (i.e., sound pedagogy)? What about *great* teaching? Don't we want teachers to be more than good; don't we want them to be great? But like great writers, great teachers are often idiosyncratic—if not downright quirky. And there's a good chance that their peculiarities contribute in some way to their greatness, a fact that makes "great teaching" almost undefinable. As soon as we identify even a single feature of great teaching, we discover an outstanding educator who may not exhibit it.

Strunk said a similar thing about great writers. "It's an old observation," he wrote, "that the best writers sometimes disregard the rules of rhetoric. When they do so, however, the reader will usually find in the sentence some compensating merit, attained at the cost of the violation. Unless he is certain of doing as well, he will probably do best to follow the rules." So it is with teaching. The best teachers may at times violate the rules of sound pedagogy for "some compensating merit," but many do so intentionally with full awareness of the underlying pedagogical principle. In short, teaching is an incredibly complex human act in which the best of the profession marshal their knowledge, skill, experience, personality, and character to educate their students.

But the truism "teaching is an incredibly complex human act" (like "teaching is an art" or "good teaching: you know it when you see it") is often unhelpful to new teachers who have yet to become the classroom masters they often long to be. New teachers (and those who train, mentor, and evaluate them) need specific, unambiguous statements that are concrete enough that these neophytes can understand them and move toward them. So rather than trying to nail down the hazy and mysterious features of *great* teaching, this book tries to establish a baseline for good—or sound—pedagogy.

Audience

This primer is specifically for those who are new to teaching and have little-to-no experience in classrooms beyond their own tenure as students. New teachers should develop good habits of sound pedagogy as early in their careers as possible, and this primer can help them start well. That said, it might also be helpful for more experienced educators. Face it: old habits die hard. Over time, experienced teachers can easily develop—quite unintentionally—ineffective pedagogical practices that do not serve their students well. Reading this text might give more experienced educators an opportunity to examine, evaluate, and improve what they do as teachers in the classroom.

Readers should be careful not to dismiss the recommendations in this book too quickly as irrelevant to their work in the classroom. For some teachers, the seemingly irrelevant portions of the text will require careful consideration and perhaps modification depending on the context (subject, grade level, etc.) in which they teach. Additionally, this primer focuses explicitly on K-12 schooling, but many of the pedagogical principles presented in this text are universal and with slight modifications may be adapted to classrooms outside of K-12 schools—i.e., preschools, colleges, and life-long learning communities.

Features

In his introduction to the 1979 edition of *The Elements of Style*, White says that his former teacher Strunk "scorned the vague, the tame, the colorless, the irresolute," and their little book was designed to be "clear, brief, bold." These three features served these authors well in their primer on composition, and so I have adopted this approach for *Tried & True*.

Clear

Throughout this text, I have used simple sentence construction whenever possible to express the basic principles of sound instruction. I have also tried to limit the use of technical jargon. Every industry has terms that allow those who work in a particular field to avoid unnecessary description and repetition. But jargon can also lead to confusion and mis-understandings, especially if those terms are poorly defined. I use some terms in this brief text that carry specific meanings within the field of education (e.g., "lesson plan," "objectives," and "assessment"), but the vocabulary included in *Tried & True* is common enough that a person with only limited experience in the field can understand and use them.

Brief

Most teachers are incredibly busy, and rookie teachers are often the busiest. As much as we would like to believe other-wise, very few new educators have time to read lengthy texts on pedagogy in order to glean a few useful instructional "tips" they need to get off to a good start in the classroom. Many practical texts on pedagogy are weighed down by detailed stories and too many examples. The examples in these kinds of books are often so grade-level and subject specific, that much of the text becomes irrelevant to one reader or another. *Tried & True* is designed to be different. The average reader should be able to complete the entire primer in an hour or two. I have kept specific examples to an absolute minimum. Readers who want more examples will have to find them elsewhere (some of these longer and more detailed texts are listed in the appendix). This primer is designed to introduce basic instructional principles and to prompt further inves-tigation and discussion among teaching colleagues: "What might this principle look like at this particular grade level or in this particular subject?" "Does it apply to my classroom?" "If so, how?" "How could I modify this technique to teach my students better?"

Bold

Again, teaching is incredibly complex, and it can be difficult to say anything meaningful about it. But education is far too important to be timid. At some point, new teachers need sound practical advice on how to do their important work. *Tried & True* does not traffic in nuance. It is unabashedly prescriptive in that it tells readers how they ought to do their job. This will no doubt lead to criticism that I have oversimplified or misrepresented teaching in some way. That's fine. As incomplete as this text may be, I am content to offer some sound practical advice to new teachers who are about to enter the most challenging job they will ever have.

Format

This primer consists of 14 imperative statements, each of which addresses an important fundamental principle of successful teaching. Following each statement, I offer some basic context for the principle so that readers will know which aspect of teaching the particular principle is meant to address. This description is followed by specific "tips" that new teachers can follow to apply this principle. I end each section with "a final thought" on the topic that helps teachers to think further about an important issue surrounding that particular principle of teaching. The sections vary in detail and length. When relevant, I include a brief example to show the principle in action.

Let's get started.

ONE

Follow the School's Mission

A SCHOOL'S MISSION DEFINES what it is, what it does, and why it does it. It is the north star to which all members of the school community can and should orientate their behavior and their work. A mission statement is a formal declaration that succinctly summarizes a school's purpose and articulates its aims, values, and commitments to which everyone associated with the school can subscribe. The mission of the school should drive *all* activities related to the school—including teaching.

A school's mission statement is most likely already in place long before any teacher is hired, so rarely are teachers involved in crafting a school's mission statement. Therefore, this text will have nothing significant to say about how to create and refine one of these statements. Of course, you should have carefully considered the mission of a particular school *prior to* your employment, and you should be clear eyed about what principles you are committing yourself to when you sign your contract. Entering into an employment contract is a serious affair, and you must be diligent to examine and understand, as much as possible, the mission statement of the school *before* you agree to teach.

So how can you deepen your understanding of the school's mission statement and the core principles behind it, and how can you use this mission to drive your teaching?

— TIPS —

Find it.

Often, the easiest way to find the mission statement is to look on the school's website. If it is not listed front-and-center on the homepage, then it is often listed under the "about" tab. You should be able to find the mission statement at or near the front of the faculty handbook or other school documents outlining policy. If the mission is not clearly labeled, you should be able to recognize it by its language. Most mission statements will include words related to knowing things (e.g., knowledge, understanding, and wisdom). They often also refer to the skills that students will acquire (e.g., "learning how to learn" or "a lifetime of learning"). And they will make reference to the kinds of people the students will ultimately be, in terms of their character, virtue, and values. In short, look for statements that have to do with the three H's: the "head" (knowledge), the "hands" (skills), and the "heart" (character).

Read it.

Once you have found the mission statement, read it slowly and frequently. Ask yourself what individual words mean and look up their formal definitions. Think about how these words work together within the statement to communicate the central purpose of the school. As you interact with your students and colleagues, look for places within the school where these key principles from the mission statement are clearly represented.

Discuss it.

Look for opportunities to discuss the mission statement with your colleagues, mentors, department leaders, and administrators. Deepen your understanding of the school's overall purpose by discussing it with those who have greater experience at the school. Ask experienced educators how the mission manifests itself in the daily activities of their classrooms. But avoid using the mission statement as a rhetorical club with colleagues and administrators (e.g., "But according the mission statement, you're wrong."). Instead, humbly acknowledge your inexperience and use conversations about the mission statement as an opportunity to learn and improve your own instruction.

Post it.

Schools often post their mission statements at various locations around the school (e.g., the main office, library, gymnasium, or cafeteria) to remind students, faculty, staff, parents, and guests of the school's mission. Some schools post the mission statement in each classroom. If the mission statement is not already posted in your classroom, consider adding it to the classroom décor—at the front of the room, next to the clock, above the classroom door, etc. Some students will recognize it on their own, but you can use a posted mission statement as a visual aid when explaining procedures, rules, assignments, grades, consequences, and other important features of the class to your students.

Review it.

Revisit the mission statement often, and set up a personal routine to review the statement regularly: before school each morning, at the beginning of your planning period, on Monday morning of each school week, on the first day of the month, etc. Of course, reviewing the mission statement will be much easier if you commit it to memory. Again, most mission statements are brief (at most, a short paragraph), and you would be wise to commit it to memory and recite it to yourself periodically. You can also review the mission statement with students in class. After all, students are an essential feature of the school community. Therefore, they too should be familiar with the mission statement of the school. These reviews with students could vary from a quick recitation of the mission statement at the beginning of class to a more detailed discussion of the statement's principles and how these ideas are represented in the class.

Infuse it.

Finally, if the mission statement is so central to the school community and its endeavors, then it should be infused into all that a teacher does in the classroom. Draw upon the principles of the mission statement when creating classroom rules, designing procedures, choosing materials, planning activities, formulating questions, and assessing students' work. You can include the school's mission statement on email signatures, in letters to parents, at the bottom of flyers, and on other classroom publications. In short, the mission statement should be infused as much as possible into every aspect of the classroom experience so that the teacher, students, and parents are all focused on the same goals.

A Final Thought

There is no such thing as a perfect mission statement. Indeed, you may come to recognize that the school's mission statement is flawed, misguided, or incomplete in some way. If so, speak up and encourage constructive conversations within the school community about how to improve the mission of the school. But be careful to do this in the appropriate context, at the appropriate time, and with the appropriate people. Because the ideas in the mission statement are so central to how the school operates, conversations about these concepts can easily become emotional and even contentious. Such heated interactions can lead to division within the school community, minimize the school's impact on students' learning, and ultimately tear the community apart. If you are a new teacher or simply new to a particular school, be especially cautious about instigating a revision to the school's mission statement too soon. While you may be full of energy and enthusiasm to improve the school by refining or redesigning its mission, your inexperience should remind you to pause, to consider that you may not see the school within a larger context, and to defer to those who have proven themselves at the school over a longer period of time.

TWO

Lead the Students

E VERY CLASSROOM HAS norms, and your success
as a teacher will depend heavily upon your willingness
and ability to embrace the responsibility for establishing
and maintaining those norms. Students need teachers to be
mature adults who take responsibility for creating a positive
and well-ordered classroom. Everyone associated with the
school—administrators, school board members, parents,
your colleagues, and even your students—expects you to do
this, and when you don't lead, the students suffer.

The school community gives you the authority to lead
in the classroom because your knowledge and character are
superior to that of your students. This does not mean that you
must be omniscient and morally perfect—even your students
know this is impossible. In fact, some of your students may
know much more than you do about particular topics because

of their personal interest or experience. But you should know *on the whole* more than your students about the content of the courses that you are teaching. And you should demonstrate *on the whole* much higher moral character than your students due to your maturity, experience, and education. When you don't know something, admit it and offer a plan for finding out the answer. When you fail to live up to high moral standards, you should demonstrate the appropriate way of accepting responsibility for your behavior, dealing with any impact of your moral failure, and restoring any relationships that you may have damaged.

This is the job. You *must* lead. If you are unable or unwilling to embrace your role as classroom leader or if you lack the potential to grow into that role within the first few years of teaching, you have no business being a teacher.

— TIPS —

Lead by example.

Model the kind of behavior you want to see in your students. If you want your students to be polite, courageous, organized, confident, curious, generous, honest, humble, and self-controlled, then you yourself should behave this way toward your students and everyone else in the school community—parents, colleagues, administrators, and visitors. Those teachers who constantly ignore school policies or complain about administrators, fellow teachers, or parents in front of students are doing a grave disservice to the school community. Teachers are representatives of and advocates for the school, its standards, and its mission. Of course, you may disagree with others on important issues within the school community, and those issues should be addressed. But for the sake of the students, these professional differences and disagreements should be handled professionally and in private. Never forget that your students are always watching you, even when they seem not to be. And they often learn more from what you do than from what you say. So as a teacher, you must live a life worthy of emulation.

Articulate your expectations early and often.

Too many teachers assume that students know implicitly what they must do to be successful in the classroom. But most students don't. You have an obligation to make your expectations abundantly clear throughout the entire school year. You cannot hold students accountable to standards if they do not know what the standards are. Take your time. Explain your expectations clearly and carefully. Be explicit about how the students can succeed in your classroom, and talk with your students (and parents) about why the class is structured the way that it is. You will later gain back the time you invested at the beginning of the school year if you articulate your expectations clearly and regularly.

Assign Seats.

In general, assigning seats to students is a good idea, especially for new teachers. Assigning seats does not solve all classroom management issues, but it definitely can minimize distractions and allow you and your students to focus on the lesson. Teachers who allow for open seating often think that students will appreciate this gesture and will therefore give them more attention and curtail their misbehavior in return. But the students' appreciation is often short-lived, and the problems that come with open seating will eventually appear. New teachers often begin the year with open seating hoping for a productive learning environment, but eventually they are "forced" to assign seats when the students are distracted and frequently off-task.

Many students do not like when they are assigned a seat, and they will often do their best to demonstrate their displeasure. But if you demonstrate confidence in the policy and explain it in a positive and rational manner, your students will often stop complaining about it and buy in to your seating plan. And although they only rarely admit it openly, some of your students actually prefer assigned seating because it allows them to focus on learning the material or it relieves them of social pressure of choosing the "right" seat. If you plan carefully, assigned seating might give students from different peer groups the opportunity to interact. There may be opportunities to allow for open seating at the highest grade levels (11th and 12th grades). But even in these cases, it would be far better to begin the year with assigned seats and give students a choice of seating only after they have demonstrated a significant period of maturity and successful work in the classroom. You should not be surprised, however, if the quality of the work decreases when you offer open seating and you must once again assign seats.

A Final Thought

Make a commitment never to be alone with a student in a room—including a classroom—with the door closed. This applies to *all* teachers regardless of their age, sex, or years of teaching experience. This personal commitment to visibility will go a long way to protect you from accusations of impropriety. If you must work with an individual student in a room, both the student and you should be seated as close to the door as possible and clearly visible to the hallway at all times. If a student enters the room when you are the only person present, politely ask the student to leave the door open or casually walk over to the door and open it yourself. This commitment to visibility is in everyone's best interest.

THREE

Establish Useful Routines

A TYPICAL CLASS PERIOD consists of hundreds of separate smaller events. Some of the most common events have very little direct connection to course material, but these events are absolutely necessary for the class to function successfully. The number and kinds of events can depend upon the subject matter, the grade level, and the maturity of the students. Common K-12 activities for students include entering the classroom, submitting homework, sharpening pencils, requesting a bathroom pass, volunteering an answer, passing papers, asking a question, cleaning up, throwing away trash, talking with classmates, getting a drink, packing up materials, exiting the classroom, and scores of other activities. All of these common classroom activities present the possibility for students to get off track and waste precious classroom time.

In order to manage the classroom efficiently so that the students are free to focus on the content of the lesson, design a series of steps for each common classroom task that students can easily follow. The number of steps for the routine depends upon the nature and complexity of the task, but each should be as simple and straightforward as possible. When successfully implemented, these routines should run smoothly in the background, and they should allow both you and your students to focus on the subject matter of the course. It is not entirely necessary for you to make a procedure for every activity in the classroom—only those activities that are most common and/or most likely to distract students from the lesson.

The long-term focus of implementing routines should be the cultivation of good character and development of productive habits in students that will serve them throughout their entire lives. But in the short term, routines should allow you to maximize student learning because these routines provide students with clear direction on how they can successfully accomplish particular classroom tasks. Whether your students express this to you openly or not, most detest ambiguous classroom expectations, and they appreciate when you clearly articulate this information.

— TIPS —

Begin well.

You can implement a new routine at any time (especially if a particular need arises), but the best time to introduce as many classroom routines as possible is during the first few days of the school year. Resist the temptation to rush through an explanation of these routines in order to get to the subject matter of the course. The time you invest in introducing, explaining, and reinforcing your classroom routines from the very beginning of the year will easily be gained back in the following days and weeks because the classroom will be operating much more smoothly and efficiently than it would have been otherwise.

Take it slow.

Start by identifying the particular common classroom task you want to address, and then carefully describe the routine for completing that task. With older students, it might be wise to give the rationale for each routine, but this is not always necessary. Next, demonstrate the routine step-by-step in order to show students what it looks like to accomplish it successfully. Then ask a couple of students to demonstrate the routine from beginning to end and comment on their ability to complete it fully and successfully. If the students are unsuccessful at demonstrating the routine, go back and reteach the routine highlighting the steps where students' attempts were incomplete or unsuccessful. The time invested in the routine will depend on the number and complexity of the steps in the routine and perhaps on how often the particular classroom task occurs in class. All classroom routines should be presented in this manner. Such an effort will require an incredible amount of patience from you, but again, it will be well worth it.

Be vigilant.

Don't assume that once you have introduced, explained, and practiced the routine, your work is over. In fact, the most challenging part of using classroom routines comes immediately after this. In the first few days and weeks of the school year, be vigilant to watch that students are successfully following the classroom routines, and be willing to reteach and practice any particular routine when you think your students need it. In the early weeks of the school year, schedule time periodically (e.g., each Monday) to revisit important or easily-neglected routines. All of this might sound tedious and juvenile, but this careful approach will absolutely be worth it in the long run. Most of your students want to know how to succeed in your class, and they will appreciate your extra effort and attention to make things clear.

Revise when necessary.

Sometimes the routines that you put in place do not work as you originally planned, or certain routines simply prove to be poorly designed. In such cases, don't try to hold on to any bad routines. The right thing to do is to admit to your students that the routine did not work as you had planned and that you need to replace it with a different routine that will hopefully lead to a more efficient learning environment. Most students will appreciate your honesty and humility in this matter, and they will most likely buy into the new and improved routine.

A Final Thought

Don't reinvent the wheel. Ask more experienced teachers what routines they use in their classrooms to accomplish common tasks. Beg, borrow, and steal from those teachers. You will quickly discover that some of the routines work rather well in your classroom, and others do not. Some may require you to modify them for your particular situation, while others you may have to abandon completely. Then you might want to ask an administrator to look over your classroom routines, and ask for feedback. After all, you may at times need administrative support when dealing with students and their parents, and it is much easier for school leaders to support you when your routines have been vetted by your administrators. You will often find these administrators to be great allies in potentially difficult situations if they know that your classroom routines are closely aligned with school policy.

FOUR

Define Expected Behavior

UNLIKE ROUTINES ASSOCIATED with particular classroom activities, rules describe how students should behave in the classroom. In this way, rules define what appropriate behavior looks like at *all* times. Most of your students will follow these rules if your expectations are realistic and fair. Students' willingness to follow the rules depends in no small measure on their perception of 1) how thoughtful you are when you design the rules, 2) how committed you are when you explain the rules, and 3) how consistent and impartial you are when you enforce the rules. Much of the above advice regarding the introduction, implementation, and supervision of routines also applies to rules.

Some teachers distribute the classroom rules as part of a course syllabus at the beginning of the school year and ask students (and sometimes parents) to sign a document confirming that they have read the classroom rules and agree to follow them. Such efforts are perfectly acceptable, and they may even help you (particularly with parents) when students fail to follow the rules. But don't assume that collecting a signed copy of classroom rules from each student will make classroom management significantly easier. The effectiveness of rules will ultimately depend on your willingness to teach the rules carefully at the beginning of the school year and then your ability to hold students accountable through consistent enforcement.

— TIPS —

Keep the list short.

Your list of classroom rules should be brief: three to six rules should be sufficient. The longer the list, the more difficult it will be for your students and you to remember. Each rule should be broad enough to capture a variety of related student behaviors within a single statement, but it should also be focused enough so that students will easily recognize its application in the classroom. For example, the rule "Always tell the truth" applies to verbal conversations, but it could also apply to how students complete their homework assignment or assessments. Make sure to discuss the scope of each rule when you are presenting them at the beginning of the year.

Keep each rule clear, concise, and positive.

Rules are difficult to remember if they are vague or wordy. If you want your students to remember the rules, you must articulate them in a clear and concise manner. So the rule "Always tell the truth" might be better stated "Be honest." You will have to balance clarity, brevity, and comprehensibility when creating your classroom rules. And the best rules are positive commands. Rather than focusing on correcting bad behavior, rules should lay out expectations for good classroom conduct so that students know what appropriate behavior looks like. For example, rather than having a negative rule that reads, "Don't touch other students," the rule could be stated as a positive, "Keep your hands to yourself." Notice how this rule is clear, concise, and positive.

Post the list.

If your list is short and each rule is clear, concise, and positive, then all of your classroom rules should easily fit on a standard-size poster board. Post this list of rules at the front of the room, and make certain that this list can be seen from any location in the classroom. It might be wise to post these rules next to the school's mission statement (see pp. 1–6). If your list of rules is located in an easily accessible location, you can actually use this list as a management tool. Say one of your students is doing something contrary to one of the rules, but you don't want to stop your lesson and distract the rest of the students (who are engaged in the lesson) to deal with this off-track student. Catch this student's eye (perhaps with raised eyebrow), walk over to the list of rules (maintaining eye contact with the misbehaving student), and point to the rule. It often takes some experience and practice to be able to continue the lesson and do what was described in the previous sentence. But this is a minimally intrusive way of communicating with misbehaving students and hopefully getting them back on track.

A Final Thought

Some teachers allow the students to develop—or to contribute to—rules for the class. These educators often claim that students are much more willing to follow the rules if the students have a say in what those rules are. Regardless of the age group or subject area, allowing students to develop classroom rules is a bad idea. Ultimately, you are the authority. While the students should be held accountable for their own behavior, it is you who will be held accountable to parents, administrators, colleagues, community members, and society at large for what occurs in your classroom. And you are the one who has been given the responsibility for establishing and maintaining a healthy and well-ordered learning environment. It may sound nice to include students in the rule-making process, but when it comes down to it, everyone knows you are supposed to be the one in charge. So embrace your role as classroom leader, and take responsibility for creating and establishing expected behavior through rules.

FIVE

Enforce Rules Fairly

CREATING A GOOD list of rules can be difficult, but enforcing those rules is the real challenge. As soon as you introduce and explain the rules to the class, you are responsible to make sure that the students follow them. As it was with routines, enforcing the rules will require a great deal of your attention, especially early in the year. Most teachers would much rather focus on helping students understand and appreciate the content of a course. But this is only possible if you manage the classroom well. If you have been faithfully and consistently holding your students accountable since the beginning of the year, you will eventually spend less and less of your time and energy enforcing and reteaching the rules. Eventually, you will recover any time you initially invested in introducing the rules at the beginning of the year. Of course, you will never stop enforcing the rules, but this responsibility should occupy less of your attention as the school year moves forward.

If you are unwilling to follow through on a rule, then you probably should not have made the rule in the first place. Rules provide a predictable structure to the class so that students know what behavior is expected of them and so that they can then focus on learning. If the enforcement of rules is applied inconsistently, the rules will fail to serve their purpose. Enforcing rules is part of being the classroom leader, and some general recommendations can help teachers do this effectively.

— TIPS —

Keep moving.

One of the key ingredients to a well-managed classroom is teacher mobility. You must be able to move around the room freely throughout the lesson and come into close proximity with any student in the room within a matter of seconds. Not only does teacher mobility keep students engaged in the lesson (in general, a mobile teacher is a more interesting teacher), but it also allows you to monitor your students' behavior and work better than if you were stationary throughout the lesson. You can often stop minor disruptions to the lesson simply by moving in close proximity to disruptive students without saying a word, without drawing attention to off-task students, and thereby without interrupting the flow of the lesson. Only truly bold students will continue to misbehave while you are standing close to them. And if these disruptions continue even after you have come into close proximity with the disruptive students, then you must use other more intrusive management techniques.

Use non-verbal cues.

When dealing with off-task behavior, use non-verbal cues such as eye contact, raised eyebrows, index finger on lips, a gesture toward posted rules, proximity, and a quiet tap on a misbehaving student's desk to get that student back on task. If these non-verbal cues fail to produce the desired effect, move toward the off-task students and address the misbehavior as quickly and quietly as possible. If a private conversation does not yield a desirable result, the matter will most likely require a different location (e.g., at the teacher's desk, in the hallway, or in an administrator's office) and perhaps at a different time (e.g., during recess, during lunch, or after school).

Correct privately.

In response to student misbehavior, some teachers move directly to loud, public confrontation with students because such responses are often quick, easy, and may initially get the kind of response they want. But these kinds of responses are almost always a bad idea. Not only are teachers supposed to model mature adult behavior, but the next confrontation with misbehaving students will most likely need to be at least equally loud and public—if not more so—in order to get a similar response.

Draw as little attention to off-task or misbehaving students as possible. If you manage the class well, most of your students will be working diligently, and there is no reason for you to interrupt these on-task students to deal with their misbehaving classmates. If students have interrupted the entire class with their misbehavior, you may need to move these disruptive students to a separate location (perhaps the hallway) and deal with their misbehavior in a more private setting. On some occasions, you can use some students' misbehavior as an example for the rest of the class, but you should be very cautious about doing so. There are often more effective ways for teaching students about proper behavior that do not require a public confrontation (and the potential of accompanying humiliation).

Praise publicly and prudently.

Whether they are willing to admit it openly or not, most of your students will appreciate your recognition and praise—especially if you have earned their respect. Public praise from you can go a long way to promoting positive and productive work in the classroom. That said, be careful not to praise students too much and unintentionally create the illusion that any particular well-behaved student is a "teacher's pet." This designation is often not regarded as a badge of honor among students, and well-behaved students may eventually go out of their way to misbehave in order to demonstrate to their classmates that they are undeserving of the "teacher's pet" designation. In other words, you can actually create management problems by publicly praising well-behaved students too much.

Frame consequences as choices.

Develop your consequences—or sequence of consequences— for misbehavior thoughtfully in advance and communicate those consequences clearly to students at the start of the school year. As it was with routines and rules, your consequences should be consistent with school policy, and you should take time well before the start of the school year to discuss these consequences with an appropriate administrator. In general, consequences should move from less intrusive to more intrusive. For example, you may begin by giving a verbal warning and jotting down a brief note in your notebook, then move to a longer conversation before or after school, and eventually assign students to a short detention. Frame these consequences as a choice that the students make rather than something that you are deciding to do. In other words, you should use something like this: "When *you* choose [misbehavior], then *you* choose [consequence]."

A Final Thought

At some point in your teaching career, you will have to deal with difficult students—those who choose to challenge and defy your authority at every turn. It can be useful to try to understand what lies behind the student's behavior, but this is not always possible. Either way, you would be wise to seek out the advice of more experienced colleagues who have spent years—if not decades—dealing with students. New teachers are often apprehensive to ask for this kind of advice because they don't want to appear weak, ignorant, or incompetent. But asking for advice from a wise colleague—especially on an issue such as dealing with difficult students—is actually a sign of maturity as an educator. If possible, speak to experienced teachers who have had the particular student in a lower grade or who currently have the student in a different subject. Don't waste time in these conversations complaining or venting about the difficult students. Rather, focus on getting valuable practical advice on how you can minimize students' misbehavior and get these students back on the right track in the classroom. If you don't know which experienced teachers to speak to, ask an administrator for a recommendation. Most good administrators know which teachers are best at handling difficult students.

SIX

Include Parents Regularly

F OR ANY CONSEQUENCE beyond a verbal warning, you should inform the appropriate administrator and perhaps the student's parents. Unless the school has another mechanism for informing parents of student misbehavior, the best method of communicating with parents is a telephone call. For most new teachers, the first few telephone calls that you make to parents can be difficult. But most parents will appreciate the time you take to call, and they will be helpful if they believe that you respect their authority as parents and you are focused on helping their child to succeed in school.

If you experience repeated frustration with a particular student, you may be tempted to vent to parents or blame them (e.g., "You won't believe what your child did today!"). This is a mistake. Make sure that you have had time to think about the student's misbehavior in a quiet, calm, and productive way.

If you are unsure about what to do next, seek out an experienced colleague or administrator who can give you sound advice about what to do next. Then formulate a specific plan for dealing with the student's misbehavior and for getting the student back on-task and productively involved in the class. Beyond that, here are some tips to help your conversation with parents go smoothly.

—TIPS—

Be respectful.

Remember that as a school teacher you are acting *in loco parentis* (in the place of the parent), but you are not to replace the parent. As a teacher, you are a resource to help parents educate their children. Never forget that in most cases, parents know more and care more about their own children than you do. This parental love may be difficult to believe sometimes from what you see and hear, but you must respect it.

Speak confidently.

Early in your teaching career, you may feel hesitant to state your position boldly due to your limited experience. This makes perfect sense, and overconfidence can be a problem for a small percentage of new teachers. But most new educators err in the other direction by being too timid with parents about what is going on in the classroom. You must carefully consider your actions and their consequences, seek advice from superiors and colleagues, and then speak confidently to parents about how you are going to move forward.

Focus on solving problems.

When calling home, look for opportunities to tell parents that you want the best for their child. Again, this is not the time or place to vent your frustration. Be clear with parents that their child is making choices that interfere with his or her education and the education of others. Describe clearly the steps you plan to take in order to move forward in a positive direction. Tell parents that you want to provide their child with the best possible education and that you are going to do your part to help their child succeed. Most parents will want to join you in this noble pursuit because this is what they want for their child, too.

Keep it brief.

While some situations require longer conversations over the phone or in person, most calls should be completed in less than ten minutes. The three basic steps for calling home are 1) identifying the problem, 2) outlining a solution, and 3) asking for any questions or comments. (Note: you may want to write these steps on a notecard and have it in front of you as you make the call.) Remember, time is precious—for parents and for you. It is easy to get bogged down in these conversations by unrelated and unimportant details. But you need to stay focused on the task at hand. If your calls to parents begin to take up too much of your time, you will be tempted to shy away from calling home in order to protect your schedule.

End on a hopeful and positive note.

If possible, find something—*any*thing—to tell parents that their child is good at or has done well. If you are truly observant, you can often find something positive to say about your students—even those who frequently misbehave and cause problems in class. Parents will see that no matter how difficult the situation has become, you are not going to give up on their child, and you remain focused on helping the student succeed. If authentic, these positive comments can encourage them to support your efforts in the classroom. You may end up recruiting parents to be incredibly useful allies if you remain positive and hopeful about their child's future.

A Final Thought

Don't wait for bad things to occur before you call home. Connect regularly with parents about positive things, too. In fact, it might be helpful to make at least one positive telephone call for every "problem" phone call you make. Or challenge yourself to make at least one celebratory phone call per week for the entire school year. For a class of twenty students, you will average about two positive calls per student per year. To help with these positive calls, keep track of special episodes or events in class when students do exceptionally well on a homework assignment, project, test, or activity. Jot down curious questions or insightful comments that your students make, and then use them when you call their parents. Make sure to keep track of which parents you have called and when. Positive calls can be especially important for parents whose students regularly get into trouble. These parents will be pleasantly surprised when they learn that you are calling about something their student did well, rather than something they did poorly.

SEVEN

Plan Lessons Purposefully

YOU MAY THINK that you can teach with little to no planning. In fact, you may have even had an experience when you didn't have time to prepare, and your performance went surprisingly well—perhaps even better than if you had spent hours preparing for it. You might be tempted to conclude that careful planning is simply a waste of time. But experienced educators know that when it comes to teaching, it is always better to put in the time developing a plan. In short, "winging it" is a bad idea. You will rue the day you decided not to invest sufficient time developing a plan for each of your lessons, and you may ultimately end up spending days and maybe even weeks backtracking through the curriculum in an effort to correct errors and fill in gaps in your students' understanding—all because you did not take time to plan well.

— TIPS —

Choose wisely.

You can't teach everything. There is simply too much to know and too little time to teach it. Planning involves choosing. This means that you must include some things and exclude others. To make these decisions, you must have some knowledge of what the students already know, what they are capable of learning now in order to move forward in their understanding, and what they will need for future learning. Do what you can to learn about your students. Ask teachers who have taught these students before. Find out what was taught to these students in previous years. Then choose the material that these students need most, and focus relentlessly on teaching that material well.

Focus on student learning.

Covering the material is not the same thing as teaching it. You can spend time talking about the content, but if your students haven't learned it, then you haven't really taught it. When planning, write out a specific statement (or two) about what you want the students to know, to do, or to experience by the end of that particular lesson. Most educators call this statement an *objective*. Then shape your lesson in such a way so that your students can have the greatest chance to be successful in meeting this objective. The lesson objective is your north star for that particular lesson in that everything in the plan should be focused on moving the students toward this goal. Writing good objectives takes practice and experience. Here are some basic examples:

- The students will be able to name the first six presidents of the United States.
- The students will create a basic outline for their essay on *Jane Eyre*.
- The students will be able to describe five important differences between plant cells and animal cells.

Some teachers may reject the idea of developing objectives because they think they are too constricting. But without an objective, teachers can easily get off track and pursue unproductive "rabbit trails" that will ultimately prohibit them from offering a rich and well-ordered classroom experience for their students. For most educators (*especially* those who are new to teaching), it is a good idea to state clearly what successful completion of the lesson looks like.

Chunk the material meaningfully.

When our minds get inundated with a steady stream of information, we can easily experience a cognitive overload of our short-term memory. If this happens, learning becomes much more difficult if not impossible. Most people have an easier time remembering new information if it is divided into smaller, more meaningful groups or *chunks*. In fact, the human mind often tries to do this kind of "chunking" automatically. This is most likely why telephone numbers, credit card numbers, and other commonly used longer number sequences are divided up into groups of three or four numbers. Chunking related information together reduces the "cognitive load" on our short-term memory. One of your jobs as a teacher is to manage the flow of new information and to make sure that students continue to engage with the material in the lesson. One of the most effective ways of doing this is to divide the material into meaningful and manageable parts and then teach those parts.

Order the content for greatest impact.

Some subjects have their own natural order. For example, history lends itself to a chronological presentation in which earlier events come before later ones, whereas mathematics and modern languages are often arranged developmentally (simple-to-complex) or procedurally (step one, step two, step three, etc.). This is not to say that these subjects must be presented in particular ways. Indeed, there are various ways to order the content within a particular field of study. But paying attention to the internal logic of the subject and doing your best to tap into this order while planning will make the material easier to remember, and it will ultimately have a greater impact on student learning.

Anticipate challenges.

Some concepts are more or less difficult to understand than others, and they may take more or less time to teach. In other words, don't assume that each new concept can be added to students' understanding at a uniform pace. Part of your job as the teacher is to review the content in light of the students you have to teach and look for hurdles and pitfalls that may trip them up. You will need to budget more or less time in the lesson to a particular concept depending on its complexity and its difficulty for your students.

Stay well ahead of your students.

Most of the time, you will be assigned to teach material that you already know. But sometimes, you may be asked to teach something (e.g., a skill, a book, a procedure, an idea) that you have forgotten or that you never learned in the first place. While this situation is not ideal for you or your students, it can be common, especially in the first years of teaching. While it would be best if you had learned all the material that you are responsible for prior to the start of the school year, this expectation is unrealistic. The next best thing is to stay a few months or weeks ahead of the students so that you have at least some perspective on the content of the course. If you are only days (or worse, one day) ahead of your students, you may ultimately waste instruction time by going back and correcting errors with students that could have been avoided if you had more insight on the entire course and beyond.

A Final Thought

Be careful not to hold too tightly to your plan. If you have invested a lot of time and energy in your plan for a particular lesson, you may be tempted to follow the plan slavishly, regardless of what occurs in class. If this happens, you may actually miss out on teachable moments that you never could have anticipated no matter how thoughtful or careful you were. Experienced teachers know that the best approach to planning involves a "loose grip"—adequately planning for each and every lesson, but not sticking too slavishly to that plan. Be flexible enough in your planning to recognize unforeseen opportunities in class and modify your lesson accordingly. You will recognize that this "loose grip" approach to designing and implementing a lesson is the most effective approach to planning. This flexibility in planning and teaching develops naturally over time with more experience in the classroom, but from the very beginning of your career, learn to plan each class with a "loose grip" in mind.

EIGHT

Begin and End Lessons Well

LIKE A WELL-STRUCTURED essay, your lesson plan should have at least three distinct parts: an opening, a body, and a conclusion. What occurs within these parts can vary somewhat, but for the sake of your students, you should keep a predictable and effective structure for most lessons. The opening and the conclusion of the lesson are somewhat similar. Both are often the shortest parts to the lesson, typically only lasting for about three to five minutes each. And both the opening and the closing should include a *review* of what was learned in the past and a *preview* of what is to be learned in the future.

Review is one of the most powerful pedagogical practices available to teachers, but sadly, many educators underuse it. One of the primary reasons for absence of review in many lessons is that most K-12 educators already feel that they have too much content to deliver and too little time to deliver it. The idea of taking precious time to go over previously presented material seems like a waste for most teachers. But remember your success in the classroom as a teacher depends not upon what you cover but upon what your students understand and remember.

Students need to be exposed to material multiple times for them to remember it long term, so you should review the previous day's material at the beginning of a lesson and review the current lesson's material at the end. But you should also regularly revisit previously presented material weeks and even months after you originally introduced it to your students if you want them to own it. If you don't do this kind of regular periodic review of previously presented material, you should not be surprised when your students cannot remember it.

— TIPS —

Prime the pump.

Some teachers like to use a warm-up activity *before* the opening of the lesson. This warm-up activity can have some connection to yesterday's lesson, last night's homework, or today's lesson. Some teachers use warm-up activities that their students can complete independently—such as a brief quiz, puzzle, or trivia question—while the teacher takes care of attendance, etc. Other teachers may choose to do a collective warm-up activity, like naming states and capitals, reciting a short poem, or singing a song. Warm-up activities can be a useful way to get students focused and ready to learn. The pace of the warm-up activity should be brisk, and the entire activity should be completed in a matter of minutes. The success of the activity often depends upon the teacher's ability to make it a part of the regular daily classroom routine.

Review previous lessons.

The opening is different from the warm up. In the opening of the lesson, review the content from yesterday's lesson or other previous lessons that may be relevant to today's objectives. By reviewing this previously learned content, you help your students to solidify yesterday's material. You will also help students remember the knowledge, skills, and experience that they will need to engage with and understand the *new* knowledge, skills, and experience in today's lesson. The best reviews often include more questions than statements. Ask students to recall and state important ideas relevant to the day's lesson. When you review at the beginning of the lesson, you help students to draw upon relevant prior knowledge, to create a ready-to-use framework for understanding new material, and to strengthen connections between old and new ideas.

Preview today's lesson.

The opening should also include a preview of the material that will be presented in the body of today's lesson. This preview should be similar to your objectives for today's lesson, but these statements should be framed in language that your students can understand and will often be less formal than the objective you wrote for yourself in your lesson plan. The central purpose of the preview is to let your students know where they are headed in today's lesson and what they are going to be doing to get there. In this preview, be explicit with your students about the structure of the lesson so that your students have a useful mental "road map" and a destination for the entire lesson.

Review today's lesson.

The closing of the lesson should be similar to the opening in that it should include a review and preview. While you should check your students' understanding throughout the lesson (more on that later), the review at the end of the lesson is a final—and perhaps more extensive—check to make sure that your students have met the objectives of the lesson. As in the opening, use questions more than statements in this review because asking students to put important ideas into their own words is often one of the best ways to check if they truly understand. Summing up an entire lesson in a few brief moments comes with a risk. These brief summaries may encourage students to oversimplify difficult and complex concepts with inaccurate, incomplete, or naïve conclusions. Be mindful of this and remind your students that they have taken another step in understanding the subject matter of the course, but that there is still more to learn.

Preview future lessons.

After looking back to the current lesson's objectives in the review, encourage students to look ahead with a very brief preview of the next day's lesson. This preview can be as long and detailed as time allows for. In this preview, you should pique your students' curiosity about the next day's lesson and begin to help them form a mental framework for it. This brief preview is an investment for the next lesson with the hope that some of these ideas will work on the students' mind— most likely, subconsciously—until your class is able to meet together once again.

A Final Thought

Repetition is closely related to review, and the two often occur simultaneously. One of the best ways to review a concept is to repeat it. When students repeat something over and over, it has a way of sticking in their minds. And there are plenty of things worth repeating: the multiplication tables, Lincoln's Gettysburg Address, Newton's Laws, the 50 states and their capitals, musical notes on a scale, Hamlet's "To be or not to be" soliloquy, the Preamble to the U.S. Constitution, the elements of the periodic table, Lewis Carroll's "Jabberwocky," etc. Some critics vilify repetition and mischaracterize it as "drill and kill," assuming that repeating something automatically leads to boredom. But repetition is one of many effective pedagogical tools that teachers can draw upon to help students learn and remember long term, especially if that repetition occurs periodically over an extended period of time. And serious educators would never believe that repetition *alone* should be used in the classroom, nor would they assume that repetition should be done in a dry and mechanical way. Those who disparage repetition should ask themselves what they would do if they needed to remember a phone number, a grocery list, or the name of a new acquaintance. My guess is that they would repeat these items over and over again. Why? Because regardless of the criticism, repetition works.

NINE

Show and Tell

THE IDEA OF teaching to students' "learning styles" is incredibly popular and commonly accepted among many educators. The nature and number of these learning styles varies widely depending on the source, but most teachers assume that there are at least three learning styles: visual learning (seeing), auditory learning (hearing), and kinesthetic learning (touching). By far the two most commonly referenced learning styles are visual and auditory. Most cognitive psychologists, however, are far more skeptical of teaching to learning styles as a pedagogical approach. There is far greater consensus that the material itself—not the learning style or preference of the student—should drive how the material should be presented.

That said, there is evidence that when teachers add *visual* representations (showing) with auditory explications (telling), the presentation of material becomes even more compelling and memorable for students. In other words, don't just show or tell; show and tell. Cognitive psychologists refer to this pedagogical method as "dual coding."

— TIPS —

Speak clearly.

You should require your students to give you their attention and listen as well as they can. But as the teacher, you have an obligation to speak clearly enough so that all of the students who are listening well can hear and understand what you are saying. This means that you must find the appropriate volume for your voice and rate for your speech. It also means that you must articulate your words in a way that is sufficiently intelligible for your students. Avoid speaking to the dry-erase board; turn and face the students when you are talking to the class. Project your voice toward them. And above all, slow down—especially when making a central point of the lesson, reading aloud a difficult passage, explaining an assignment, demonstrating a complicated process, reciting an elegant line of poetry, etc. Your students' learning should never suffer because they cannot hear or understand you.

Write clearly.

Similar principles apply to your writing. Although teachers are quick to criticize their students for unintelligible writing, many educators—especially those in the upper grades—give themselves excuses for sloppy writing. But remember: teachers should lead by example. If you want your students to use good handwriting, you must demonstrate the same for them on written feedback, on notes to students, but especially on the board at the front of the classroom. If you have poor handwriting, work on it. Get an elementary handwriting book, and retrain yourself to form the letters correctly. Then practice writing on the board. Invest your time and effort in communicating clearly. You should also consider writing key words, phrases, figures, and examples on the board before class begins because it is often more difficult to write clearly while you are teaching. Again, the students who want to understand should be able to understand, and the quality of your handwriting should never be an impediment to their learning.

Use visual aids.

Visual aids include objects, maps, diagrams, charts, photographs, sketches, and even videos that illustrate graphically the concept you are trying to teach verbally. Again, use the visual representation of the material *while* you are giving the verbal description. When appropriate, students should have opportunities to create or complete their own visual aids, but the students' graphic organizers should not replace the visual aids that you use as teacher to make the content understandable and memorable. Your visual aids should not be distracting, confusing, or unnecessarily complex. Your goal when using visual aids is not to entertain or amuse your students, but to help them learn.

Tell stories.

Many subjects include abstract concepts that are disassociated with specific instances. Part of your job as a teacher involves linking these abstract concepts to specific and concrete examples so that students can understand. One of the best ways of providing concrete examples for abstract concepts is to tell stories. Telling stories is an incredibly powerful way of communicating ideas between human beings. Because stories often follow a familiar path (or arc), there is a built-in mental framework for students to arrange new knowledge. Human beings often find stories more interesting than other means of delivering information, so stories are often more engaging and memorable to us.

Think about how you can communicate the material as close to a story as possible without misrepresenting it. For subjects such as literature and history, the use of stories in teaching is natural because the content already contains many essential elements of a story: characters, conflict, chronology, causality, complications, etc. But even those subjects that one would not naturally associate with stories—such as mathematics, science, and modern languages—can also be presented in a way that draws upon these common narrative elements. Look for ways in which the subject's natural features are similar to those features commonly found in a story. For example, the procedural steps of a mathematical equation or science experiment may *resemble* the chronology of a story. If you can describe that procedure like a story, the students may have a better chance of remembering it. Your job is to look for features within the content that are common to stories and to use those features to increase students' understanding.

Use worked examples.

One of the most effective forms of demonstrations is called "worked examples," step-by-step modeling of a task (e.g., drawing a face, balancing a chemical equation, singing a scale, writing a paragraph, or outlining a geometric proof) in which you (the expert) show your students (the novices) how to accomplish a task successfully from the beginning to the end. And while you may pepper your instruction with predictive and prior-knowledge questions in order to engage and encourage your students, you will do most of the work during this stage while your students watch, listen, and learn. Depending on the complexity of the material and the prior knowledge of the students, you may need to offer multiple demonstrations of the material. In most cases, your involvement will decrease as the lesson moves along and your students begin to develop the ability to understand the material for themselves.

Alternate worked examples and independent practice.

With certain elements of the curriculum, students need the opportunity to practice or apply what they have learned. Traditionally, this was accomplished by a three-step process: teacher input, guided practice, and independent practice. There is some solid evidence to suggest that this traditional teaching process can be improved by altering it slightly. Rather than having extended periods of teacher input, then guided practice, and finally independent practice, you can alternate your instruction between worked examples and student practice over the course of the entire lesson. This process moves students incrementally and progressively through the material by alternating between the teacher's presenting clear, step-by-step, written-out solutions to problems and the students' practicing the new material by completing similar, related problems for themselves.

Move around the classroom.

As stated earlier, teacher mobility is an important part of managing the classroom well because it is easier to observe students and communicate with them if you are moving in and around them. But teacher mobility is also an important technique for keeping students engaged in the lesson. Remember: all things being equal, a mobile teacher is more interesting than a stationary one. And there is no rule that says a teacher must remain in one location at the front of the classroom. Teachers should only be limited in their mobility by the resources they need (e.g., a lab table, visual aids, and dry-erase boards) for teaching and the congestion of the room. From the first day of classes, demonstrate to your students that you will be moving around the classroom when you teach. If you do this, they will get used to your movement around the room as a normal part of your teaching.

A Final Thought

As stated earlier, repeated practice can be an incredibly valuable tool for teachers who want to challenge their students and give them the best possible opportunities to learn. Plenty of important academic skills (e.g., reading fluency, multiplication tables, and poetry recitations) become automatic when students practice them over and over. But this is not true for all academic work. In fact, *more* work (quantity) can be *less* effective (quality) in helping students learn if the work grinds the students down and wears them out. So with certain material, *less* work can ultimately be *more* effective if the work is specifically targeted at helping the students understand the content of the lesson. Ultimately, these kinds of pedagogical decisions will be based upon your knowledge of students, your familiarity with the material that you teach, and your experience in the classroom.

TEN

Ask Good Questions

A QUESTION IS AN incredibly powerful pedagogical tool. Questions can clarify and solidify what students know, but they can also help students learn how to think and reason about that knowledge too. Well-crafted questions should encourage students to draw upon factual knowledge, to examine relationships between ideas, to consider available evidence, and to formulate well-reasoned positions. In other words, good academic questions require students to do more than share their opinions or feelings.

The kind of engagement with questions and answers described below is extremely difficult to do well. It often takes teachers years—if not decades—of experience to use questions smoothly, efficiently, and effectively. The only way for teachers to develop this skill is to practice. Here are some tips to help you practice well.

— TIPS —

Use various types of questions.

Teachers should not rely exclusively on one type of question; rather, they should use a variety of question types that help the students to meet the lesson objectives and the goals of the course. There are many different types of questions. Think of questions along a continuum with "closed-ended" questions on one end and "open-ended" questions on the other. More closed-ended questions often require students to give shorter, straightforward, factual answers, and they typically begin with words like *who, what, where,* and *when*.

- Who was the first person to cross the Atlantic Ocean in an airplane?
- What is the atomic weight of copper?
- Where is the Nile River located?
- When was George Washington born?

More open-ended questions often require students to give longer, more complex and detailed replies that demand greater time and reflection of the students. Open-ended questions can easily lead to further discussion and debate, and they typically begin with words like *how* and *why*.

- How can I find the length of the hypotenuse of a right triangle?
- Why did the League of Nations ultimately fail?
- How do you know an apple is a fruit?
- Why did Elizabeth Bennet reject Mr. Darcy's first marriage proposal?

Some teachers rely heavily on a single type of question, and typically those questions demand little more than information recall. Now, knowledge is incredibly important, and analytical thinking is best developed in the context of real knowledge. But students learn to think best when teachers use a wide variety of question types.

Formulate important questions before class.

Most teachers find it difficult to use questions effectively in class, especially if they are trying to come up with questions spontaneously. It is a good idea to write out key questions while planning. Even if you do not use these prepared questions or if you modify these questions significantly based on how the lesson progresses, the process of formulating questions and answers beforehand will often help you to pose more insightful and targeted questions during instruction. You may also want to list or provide an outline of potential answers so that you have an idea of what you want to hear from your students as a result of your questions.

Display important questions for students.

The previous section briefly presented show-and-tell ("dual coding") as an effective way of presenting new material to students. This principle also applies to asking questions. Allow your students to see (on the board at the front of the room, on a handout, etc.) for themselves the most important questions while you pose them to the class verbally. These visual cues will allow your students to see the words and structure of the questions, and this additional visual element will most likely lead to better understanding of the question and ultimately to better quality answers and discussion.

Ask students to write out and/or discuss answers before sharing.

In order to get better answers from your students, add an additional step to your questioning technique, especially for more open-ended questions. Ask students to write out an answer in a notebook, on a worksheet, or on a dry-erase board before you call on particular students for answers. Not only does this give students a little extra time to collect their thoughts, but it also gives all students the opportunity to attempt an answer privately before you ask them to give an answer publicly. You can also add in a few moments for a brief conversation between classroom partners after you pose the question but before you call on individual students for an answer. In order to improve efficiency and to minimize distractions, you should already have designated (at the beginning of the year, the semester, the marking period, or the week) student partners who are in close proximity to each other in the classroom. The time to discuss the answer between partners will depend upon a variety of factors (e.g., the complexity of the question, the prior knowledge of the students, etc.) but in general, the conversation between these partners should be as brief and focused as possible. Call on one student or both students to provide an answer based on what the partnership came up with together. Many students often feel more willing to share an answer if it represents more than just their own thinking. You can also give students some time to consider the question independently prior to partnering up for a brief conversation. This technique is often called "think-pair-share," as in 1) *think* about possible answers by yourself, 2) *pair* up with your partner for a brief conversation about possible answers, and 3) *share* your answer with the rest of the class when prompted by the teacher.

Call on both volunteers and "victims."

Sometimes teachers will answer their own questions, but most often, the answer will come from students. By far, the most common approach to in-class questions looks like this: you ask a question, you wait for one or more of your students to raise their hands, and you select a volunteer to answer the question. Calling on volunteers can be effective, but it has some drawbacks. For example, if you rely only on volunteers, you should not be surprised if the same small group of students answer all of the questions. And typically that small group is composed of those students who are already the most knowledgeable, most skilled, and most outgoing members of the class. In fact, the students who know the least or are least engaged in the lesson (i.e., those who need the most help) know they are "safe" from being asked questions by teachers who solely rely on volunteers. But you are responsible for the education of *all* your students in your classes, not just the smartest and boldest.

Other teachers choose to call primarily on "victims" (i.e., anyone in the class whether they have a hand up or not) to answer questions. There is an obvious benefit to this approach. Because students know that they could be called upon, there is a greater chance that students will be much more engaged with the lesson. In the first few days of the school year, it might be difficult to get the students to respond with an answer, but you should stick with it. Over the course of the semester or year, the students will be much more engaged and (hopefully) more productive. As you begin to know your students' abilities and personalities better, you will be better able to choose the best victim for each question.

Ultimately, it is probably best to call upon *both* volunteers and victims intermittently. By calling on volunteers, you are giving those students who have worked diligently a chance to prove it, and by calling on victims, you will encourage all students to be involved in the lesson and to be prepared to give an answer.

Be patient.

Many teachers fail to give their students the time necessary to think carefully, gather relevant ideas, and come up with a thoughtful and coherent answer. Instead they pose the question and then immediately call on students. There is a sequence of steps for asking questions in class that works well for most questions—and it is especially important for more open-ended questions—but it will require you to be patient. First, prepare the students for your question. Tell the class that you are going to pose a question, and tell them that you *don't* want them to raise their hands or call out an answer. Second, ask the question slowly and carefully. If the question is long or complex, you may want to repeat it a second time—or more—if necessary. (Note: you may want to tell them how many times you are going to ask the question so that the students know to pay close attention, rather than relying on too many repetitions of the question.) Third, wait. Give the students time to interpret and understand the question, to think about what it means, to draw the necessary knowledge and skills, and to collect their thoughts into a meaningful reply. The failure to give students this time to think may be the most common mistake that teachers make when posing questions. Giving students time to think will often increase the quality of students' answers and may increase the number of students who are able and willing to offer a reply. Fourth, call for an answer, and then choose a student (volunteer or victim) to offer a reply. Fifth, wait *again*. Resist the temptation to respond to the given answer immediately. Whether you eventually confirm a right answer or correct an erroneous one, this additional moment or two of waiting will allow other students in the class to make their own judgment about the quality and accuracy of the first student's reply.

At this point in the question-answer sequence, you can respond to the initial answer in a wide variety of ways depending on where you want the conversation to go. You can confirm that the initial answer is correct (or incorrect) and move on to the next topic. This is the most common way to respond to students' answers, but it is not always the best. You should know that this kind of affirmation could easily end what might have been a deeper and richer discussion of ideas. You may want to ask the responding student to say more about the initial answer and to add clarity or detail to what was initially said, especially if that first reply was poorly articulated or incomplete. You may want to pose additional questions that will encourage the students to think more deeply about what was offered in the initial answer. You can also ask other students in the class to make constructive comments about the initial response or to pose their own related questions to the class.

Watch out for cop-outs.

Some students try to avoid answering question by reflexively saying, "I don't know." While it may certainly be true that your students do not know the answer to your question, this reply is often little more than an attempt to shrug off their responsibility as students to engage with the material and be proactive members of the class. At the beginning of the school year, you may want to tell your students that "I don't know" is an unacceptable response to your inquiries and that you expect something more from them. Then teach your students alternative replies that they can use to create opportunities for further discussion and learning, such as

- "Would you please repeat the question?"
- "Would you please state the question a different way?"
- "May I please try to restate your question a different way?"
- "May I please ask a clarifying question first?"
- "Would you please come back to me once I have heard from others?"

A Final Thought

Don't assume that your students' inability to answer your questions is always due to their laziness or lack of preparation. Sometimes the problem is that they do not understand the question, they don't know how to frame their answer, or they lack the prerequisite knowledge or skill. And sometimes they are asked to answer complex, open-ended questions without being given the time to think (see "be patient" above). Anticipate potential misunderstandings of your questions, and be ready to state them a different way. Make certain the students have the prior knowledge and skills to think about and answer your questions *before* you ask. And with the most important questions, make sure that you have moved your students along slowly and carefully, so that when you ask your questions, your students are primed and ready to respond in a meaningful and constructive way. In a way, posing questions is easy. The difficult part is choosing *good* questions and then making sure that your students are prepared to answer them.

ELEVEN

Lead Engaging Discussions

CLASSROOM DISCUSSIONS CAN help students think carefully about incredibly complex issues. Most classroom discussions begin with the teacher posing a broad question about an important topic and then asking the students to engage with one another in an orderly conversation about the chosen topic. The teacher then plays the role of moderator in order to keep the discussion focused, interesting, civil, and productive. When modified appropriately for the students' age and maturity, classroom discussions can be used for every subject and at every grade level.

Leading a classroom discussion is incredibly difficult, perhaps one the most challenging and exhausting activities that any teacher can do. It is especially difficult for new teachers. And because classroom discussions are often done so poorly, many so-called discussions are simply a waste of precious classroom time. Most of the problems associated with classroom discussions can be overcome by thoughtful planning and regular practice. Here are some basic recommendations for a successful discussion.

— TIPS —

Map out the journey.

Remember: the lesson objective should drive everything in the lesson. You should choose to lead a classroom discussion because it will help your students meet the specific objective of that lesson. So the objective is the destination, and now you need to lay out a series of statements and questions that you can use that will move the students toward that objective. Design a discussion "map" with certain "markers" or "gates" (e.g., questions, comments, or even facial expressions) that you would like to see or hear from your students during the course of the conversation. These markers or gates are indicators that your students are moving in the right direction (i.e., toward the lesson objective).

Anticipate problems.

Many teachers fail to lead effective discussion because they have not thought about where and how the discussion could get off course. Make sure that you think about which questions or concepts could easily sidetrack the students and lead the discussion into unnecessary or unproductive areas. Sometimes these unexpected diversions in the conversation can lead to rewarding experiences for the entire class. But more often than not, these "rabbit trails"—even when they come from the teacher—are unproductive, distracting, and ultimately a waste of time.

Choose appropriate content.

Make sure the material that you want the students to discuss provides opportunities for interpretation, disagreement, or debate. Resources that provide these kinds of engagement include stories, paintings, essays, songs, and images. If the material simply provides factual information (e.g., a collection of data, a procedure, or a summary report), don't be surprised if your students find it difficult to say anything interesting or insightful. If you want your students to think, analyze, and develop a conceptual understanding of important issues, you need to offer them content that will allow them to do this.

Prepare the physical space.

Certain classrooms layouts (e.g., traditional rows and columns or small-group "pods") make it difficult for students to engage in a whole-class discussion because participants cannot establish and maintain eye-contact with classmates. Make sure that you have arranged the physical space so that students are easily able to see and hear one another. This might mean that desks will need to be moved within the classroom. If the classroom cannot be modified, you may need to move the entire class to a different location (e.g., a library, a courtyard, or a multi-purpose room) that would be more conducive to this sort of activity.

Show students how to participate.

Don't assume that students know how to engage in a civil and productive discussion with one another about an important topic. Some (and perhaps many) of your students have never been taught what this kind of conversation should look like and why. Similar to what you do for your classroom rules and routines, you need to describe what proper participation for the discussion should look like. But more than that, you will need to model and enforce these expectations as discussion moderator. Once students learn how to participate, you may allow students to moderate the conversation, but as the authority in the classroom, you need to be ready to support the students and step in as moderator when necessary.

Start small.

Since classroom discussions are often difficult both for the teacher and for the students who lack experience, it's a good idea to start small. You might want to try a mini-discussion of about five to ten minutes that may be surrounded by other types of activities, such as lecture, demonstration, or group work. Think of this experience as an extended question-and-answer time. This may seem like a relatively short period, but if you have never led a classroom of students in an engaging conversation, five to ten minutes can be very long indeed. Once you have been successful in leading a few ten-minute mini-conversations, you can probably extend the activity to 15-20 minutes if you think it will help your students better meet the lesson objective. But unless you are somewhat of a natural at leading discussions or you have been able to perfect discussion techniques, you should probably not plan to lead a discussion longer than 30 minutes in your first few months of teaching.

Give students time to prepare.

Although they may not always show it, most students want to participate in classroom discussions. In fact, many enjoy it. The problem is often that they are simply unprepared. In other words, they have not had the time nor the opportunity to collect and organize their thoughts on the topic before the discussion. Instead, ask them to think about some pre-discussion questions that will require them to retrieve the knowledge, skills, and experiences that they will need to be active, contributing members of the discussion. Give them a few minutes to create a list of words or phrases related to the topic that they can refer to and draw upon during the discussion. If you give students the opportunity to prepare—even briefly—for the discussion, you may be surprised by how much better the conversation will be.

Give students time to reflect.

Some discussions fail to help students learn, not because of what happened during the discussion, but because of what happened after. Students often need time to reflect on and solidify what they said and heard during the discussion in order for the important and relevant points to stay in their minds. Give your students a brief post-discussion period when they can reflect on what they said and heard, and ask them to list three to five of the most important items. You can then ask them to use these items to write a summary paragraph of the discussion where they combine the items in meaningful ways. Students can volunteer to read their summaries aloud to the class in the final few minutes of the lesson, or they can submit the paragraph for a completion grade.

Learn from your successes and failures.

After a class in which you use discussion, take a few minutes to reflect on the experience. What went well? What went poorly? What should you change? What should you keep the same? If you were to do the same discussion again, how would you change it? These questions can be useful, especially if your reflection is done soon after the discussion concludes. Then come up with strategies to continue what worked and eliminate or modify what didn't. If you have a pattern of successful discussions over multiple weeks, you may want to extend your next discussion by another five minutes or so. If you are struggling to offer your students a productive discussion experience, you may need to contract it a little and go back to a more manageable time limit.

A Final Thought

Good discussion leaders are often made, not born. Certainly some teachers have natural gifts that lend themselves well to classroom discussion. But even these naturally gifted teachers often need time practicing this craft in the classroom. Begin by understanding what a good discussion looks like. The best way to do this is to observe good discussion leaders at work. If you don't know which colleagues are good at leading discussion, ask your administrators to give some recommendations. If possible, follow up your observations with a meeting so that you can ask these successful colleagues about what they do before, during, and after the classroom discussion in order to make them work. Then, try to incorporate what works for you in your own classroom instruction.

TWELVE

Use Small Groups Wisely

SMALL-GROUP ACTIVITIES ARE incredibly popular in schools today. Ideally, these activities provide students with an opportunity to work together toward a common goal with each member contributing equally (or almost equally) to the success of the entire group. In truth, small-group activities often waste precious class time because less motivated students rely on their more motivated group members to do most of the work.

Whole-class activities are almost always superior to small-group activities. When the class remains together as a large group, all of the students have direct and immediate access to the teacher at all times. And with whole-class activities, the teacher has immediate oversight of all the students. Again, small-group activities can easily waste precious classroom time, so you should design classroom activities that keep the entire class together as much as possible. That said, sometimes small-group activities (e.g., science lab) can be useful in the classroom as long as the teacher follows some basic recommendations.

— TIPS —

Make sure the students are prepared.

As it is with other activities, small-group activities often fail because students are unprepared to do the work. So make sure that your students have the prerequisite knowledge and skills that they will need to be productive in a group. It is often a good idea to have students work independently for a short time before they join their small group. Similar to a discussion, ask students to create a list of relevant words or phrases that might be used in the small-group activity. Or ask them to sketch a diagram or write a brief paragraph independently before joining the group. Then once the students are finished in their groups, they can return to their individual work (i.e., list, paragraph, diagram) and revise it accordingly.

Keep the groups small.

Groups should have the fewest number of students possible. Typically, pairs are better than three students, three students are better than four, four are better than five, etc. If small groups have too many students, it is easier for students to avoid doing work and being actively involved. Assigning specific jobs to group members in a larger group can help keep students engaged, but keeping the groups small is much better because it is easier to hold the members of a smaller group accountable for the work of the group.

Keep the activity brief.

Many small group activities fail because teachers give the students too much time to accomplish the assigned task. Often teachers know that students waste time in small groups, so they give them more time to complete the task than is really needed. It is far better to keep the small-group activity as brief as possible and then hold them accountable for what they accomplish. Some of the most productive small-group activities can be completed in five to ten minutes. Of course, the length of time of a small-group activity will depend upon grade level, subject matter, maturity of the students, and other variables. But if you are using an entire class period (or more) for small-group activities, then most likely you are wasting precious class time.

Keep the students focused.

Small-group activities also fail when teachers do not clearly articulate to the students what they are to accomplish as a group. Clearly outline to your students what they are to do as a group, how they are to accomplish the task, and what kind of product (see below) will come out of their collective effort. Depending on the age and maturity of your students, you may need to lay out specific steps that each group should accomplish on their way to the final outcome.

Hold the students accountable.

Students must be held accountable for the time they spend in a small group. The best way to do this is to require some product at the conclusion of the activity (e.g., a brief presentation, a list of ideas, a paragraph, a diagram, etc.). This product could be from the entire group, but again, some students may rely on the work of other more dedicated (or more grade-conscious) members of the group. It's far better for each member of the group to provide some product (or some part of a larger product) for which you will hold that group member accountable. You may choose to grade these products, or you may simply give each student credit for completing that portion of the work.

Circulate around the classroom.

Never assume that small-group activities afford you a break from your regular teaching duties. Just as you should move around the classroom during a lecture or discussion, you should circulate around the classroom monitoring conversation and behavior, answering questions, and providing feedback during these small group activities. Keep mobile, and move from group to group throughout the entire activity, never allowing yourself to get "stuck" longer than a moment or two with any one group. If it becomes apparent that the groups are not functioning productively and independently during the allotted time, it is often wise for you to cut the small-group activity short, bring the entire class back together, and work as a whole class.

A Final Thought

Many—though certainly not all—students like small-group activities because they often give students the freedom to interact with one another (and to share the workload). But be careful about choosing an activity simply because it appears to be popular or fun. Activities should focus on helping students learn. Yes, you should make a concerted effort to keep students interested and engaged in the lesson, but this is quite different from keeping them entertained. You will never be able to compete with what is available in media and entertainment, so stop trying. Again, the lesson objectives should drive what activities you use in the classroom, so ask yourself this question: "What activity will best allow my students to learn this material?" While teachers should look for opportunities to promote wonder and joy in the classroom, the choice of activity should never be driven by what is entertaining. Teachers must focus on student learning.

THIRTEEN

Assess Students Regularly

F OR MANY TEACHERS, assessment is the most challenging and least enjoyable part of the job. It can easily consume large quantities of teachers' time and energy, and it can become a source of conflict for teachers with students, parents, and even administrators. But assessment is a necessary and important part of teachers' work, and when it is done accurately and efficiently, it can be valuable for all involved. Basically, assessment involves measuring students' work against some standard of quality. Teachers ask students to respond to particular prompts, and then teachers must judge the students' work against what they expect their students should know or be able to do.

Think of assessment techniques along a continuum of formality: less formal on one end and more formal on the other.

Less formal assessments may include looking at students' facial expressions, watching for the nodding of students' heads, or perhaps observing a "show of hands" in response to a particular question. The advantage of these less formal assessments is that they provide you with a quick check of your students' understanding; the disadvantage is that they are not very reliable. For example, your students might easily maintain eye contact with you, smile, and nod their heads eagerly, but they may still be confused about what you have been teaching them. Moderately formal assessments may include asking students to answer closed-ended and open-ended questions aloud. These types of assessment are often more reliable than informal assessment, but less reliable than more formal ones. You can improve the reliability of these moderately formal checks by adequately sampling the class: advanced students and struggling students, vocal and quiet, those in the front of the room and those at the back, left side and right, female and male, etc. More formal assessments include asking students to respond to particular prompts in writing, to create a particular product, or to perform a particular task. One of the best tasks you can use to check students' understanding is to ask them to summarize—verbally or in writing—what they have learned in their own words. Students who claim to understand but are unable to articulate their understanding in their own words most likely do not truly understand. These more formal assessments are often more reliable measures of student understanding, but they often take more time to administer and evaluate.

— TIPS —

Use formative assessment to check understanding.

Regardless of the kind and number of activities in a lesson, you should check students' understanding periodically *throughout* the lesson. Formative (i.e., "forming" or "ongoing") assessments of student learning allow teachers to make sure that the students are following along with the instruction, moving toward the lesson objective, and ultimately growing in their understanding of the subject matter to be learned. If the students are able to answer your questions or perform a particular task, you can move forward in the lesson with relative confidence. Formative assessment should also inform teachers' moment-to-moment decisions in the classroom. If the students are unsuccessful during these periodic reviews, you should pause instruction and go back to previous points in the lesson in order to reteach particular elements. This "reteaching" may involve simply restating an earlier point, but most likely it will require you to rephrase what was said earlier, give further examples, or take an entirely different approach to teaching the content. If you do not periodically check for student understanding, the lesson may come to its conclusion and you may discover that the students were lost in the first few minutes of class, and precious time and energy were unnecessarily wasted.

Use targeted questions.

Some of the most common questions that many teachers ask to check students' understanding are some of the least effective. Visit almost any classroom at any grade level, and you will hear questions such as

- "Does everyone understand?"
- "Is anyone confused?"
- "Are there any questions?"

These vague question rarely yield the kinds of replies that will help you check understanding and identify gaps in students learning. Instead, ask targeted questions that are specific to the content of the lesson that you are teaching. You can always call for questions in a more general way ("Are there any questions?"), but only after you have determined by means of specific targeted questions that your students are following the lesson.

Use formative assessment to boost understanding.

Low-stakes assessment (e.g., a short quiz with a low point value) can help boost student understanding. In the short term, most students will be more motivated to do well on the assessment if they know they can earn points toward a course grade, even if the number of available points is small. In the long term, most students will remember the material better because they have had to bring it to mind during the assessment. Regular formative assessments that require the retrieval of previously learned material are some of the most effective ways to improve student retention.

Use summative assessment to evaluate student learning.

Use summative (i.e., "sum" or "summary") assessments *after* or at the end of an instructional period (a lesson, unit, course, etc.) in order to see whether the students have truly met the objectives or reached the intended goals. Summative assessments are usually much more broad in their scope than formative assessments. The best summative assessments sample material from across the instructional period and typically require students to bring seemingly disparate ideas together as a coherent whole. In the early stages of planning a unit and a course, think about what you will ultimately do at the end of the instructional period to assess student learning. If you have been consistently using formative assessments, your students' performance on summative assessment should not be a surprise to anyone—including you.

Use clear directions and prompts.

The goal of assessment is to measure student learning, and the quality of the assessment often depends on the quality of the directions and prompts (e.g., questions, statements, and images). The best directions and prompts avoid cluttered and confusing language. Instead, they state the expectations for the students in a way that is clear and unambiguous. Before you give the assessment to students, make sure that you read your directions and prompts slowly and carefully (preferably out loud) to yourself. Then ask yourself some questions: Based on what I know of my students and what we have done together in this class, will the students understand the directions and prompts clearly and completely? Does anything need to be added, taken out, or restated in order to communicate the expectations of the assessment to the students? Will the students who complete this assessment have any trouble interpreting and understanding what is required of them in this assessment?

Try it out.

If possible, complete your own assessment before giving it to your students. In the case of an essay and paper/project/performance, you can write or create an example to serve as a model. Of course, you should have no problem with the material on the assessment, but trying the assessment is a good way to review what the students will be required to do. As you complete your own assessment, you will often catch errors that could have led unnecessarily to student confusion or misunderstanding. And this "dry run" will allow you to see (somewhat) the assessment from the students' perspective in order to understand what students will need to do to succeed.

Help students prepare.

Left to themselves, students often choose ineffective study techniques—such as rereading the textbook, highlighting their notes, and (worst of all) cramming—because they may have experienced some short-term success in the past. But these common preparation methods are quite ineffective if the goal is long-term learning. Instead, you should create opportunities (in class and at home) for students to use more effective study techniques. Such techniques include 1) asking students to create their own summaries (in their own words) of newly presented material, 2) scheduling shorter study periods over a longer span of time, and 3) providing brief study breaks periodically so that students can refresh and refocus their attention.

A Final Thought

Preparing for assessment can be incredibly stressful for students, especially if those assessments have "high stakes" attached to them. A little anxiety can be a good thing for students because it encourages them to focus and to apply themselves. If there is little or no pressure, students tend to become unmotivated and unfocused. So pressure can be good. But too much pressure can lead to students becoming overly stressed. Part of teaching is finding the right balance between too much pressure and not enough.

FOURTEEN

Provide Constructive Feedback

F EEDBACK IS AN important part of the assessment process, and it is most effective when it is given promptly (i.e., as soon as possible after the students have completed the task), clearly (i.e., in language that the student will understand), and accurately (i.e., in relation to the previously presented expectations). Of course, it is always wise to provide an honest word of encouragement when students have performed well on an assessment. But most feedback is corrective in that it identifies and describes where and how students have not met the objective or have fallen short of the goal.

Often, written feedback is the most time-consuming part of the assessment process for teachers. Teachers often feel as though they are only doing their best for students if they are carrying home armloads of papers, workbooks, and projects to grade after school to evaluate and to write comments for each student on every assignment. But time is zero-sum. And all of this effort to provide detailed written feedback may ultimately lead to poor teaching if it pulls teachers away from other essential pedagogical tasks (e.g., reading, planning, and collecting resources) or if it unnecessarily wears them down physically, mentally, or emotionally. An exhausted teacher is an ineffective teacher. And the students will ultimately suffer. There are some things that you can do to increase the value of written feedback for students and to limit the time spent on assessment.

— TIPS —

Focus on objectives and goals.

On most students' work, teachers could provide written feedback on any number of items. This is especially true with students' responses to more open-ended prompts where they must bring together ideas in an extended format (e.g., a paper, performance, or project). But as it is with instruction, the lesson objectives or unit goals should drive assessment and the resulting feedback from teachers. Ask yourself what you want your students to know or be able to do with a particular assignment, and then focus on those specific elements when you provide written feedback. You may need to tell your students what you focused on during your assessment so that they will not assume that all unmarked portions are error-free.

Limit frequency.

Providing feedback to students is an important part of a teacher's job. A teacher's direction, advice, and support can be incredibly formative in shaping what students learn. But your time is much too valuable to examine all your students' work closely and to offer detailed written feedback on all that they complete and submit. Sometimes a quick check of students' work is sufficient. If during this review, you begin to notice common errors across multiple students' work, make a note of the problems and bring them up in the following class period.

Limit details.

When you give written feedback, do your best to limit your comments to only what is truly necessary. Of course, focusing only on specific elements will help you to be more efficient with your time. You can also use a set of symbols (e.g., letters, numbers, arrows, and shapes) with an accompanying key to communicate certain details that would have required you to write longer words, phrases, sentences, etc. Teach these symbols at the beginning of the school year as part of the class orientation process and then use them regularly throughout the academic year.

Involve students.

Teachers often do work that students could do for themselves. In fact, many students benefit from doing an intentional review of their own work and the work of classmates. Create opportunities for students to identify and mark commonly occurring errors, such as spelling, grammar, and formatting. In order to make sure that students are able to do this kind of peer review well, you will need to take time to train the students on how to do this work responsibly, and you will then need to supervise and monitor the students closely as they work.

Use collective feedback.

If students do not receive written feedback soon after submitting their work, the impact of the feedback on their learning will be limited. In other words, the longer the duration between turning it in and getting it back, the less effective the feedback will be. This can be incredibly discouraging to teachers who spends hours and hours providing written feedback on students' work. But it is helpful to realize that students of the same class often make similar errors. Sometimes it is better to review the entire class's work without writing comments directly on students' work. Instead, have a notepad next to the stack of student work and jot down notes to yourself regarding common errors that you notice while you quickly look through the students' work. The next school day (or very soon after), highlight some of the common errors that you have noticed with the entire class. Then ask the students to answer questions or rework problems where these errors were frequent. Not only will this approach save you precious time, but students will not have to wait too long for feedback.

Assign appropriate grades.

Schools use grades as a means of communicating to students, parents, and others about how much students have learned. Grades are not the only means of communicating this information, but they are certainly one of the most common. Although the specific application and understanding of what each grade means often varies from teacher-to-teacher (even within a given school and among teachers at the same grade level), there are certain general expectations about what specific letter grades mean quantitatively (numerical) and qualitatively (descriptive). This book will say little more about this topic than to provide a very basic quantitative and a qualitative description associated with each of the most common letter grade:

Letter	Quantitative	Qualitative
A	100-90%	Excellent
B	89-80%	Good
C	79-70%	Fair
D	69-60%	Struggling
F	59% or below	Poor

A Final Thought

If you are going to spend so much of your precious time and energy providing written feedback to your students, make certain that the feedback will help your students learn. The best way to promote the efficacy of your comments is to ask the students to do something with the comments. Ask your students to respond to the comments in writing or to make changes to their work. Without this effort on behalf of your students, the hours you spend providing written feedback on your students' work is almost certainly time wasted.

Conclusion

TEACHING IS INCREDIBLY complex. New teachers who expect perfection from the start of their teaching careers will be sorely disappointed. Although some educators come to the profession with incredible natural abilities, the best teachers—like the best chefs, athletes, and artists—take years of learning, focus, and practice to hone their craft. New teachers should recognize their shortcomings, look for alternative methods by observing their experienced colleagues, try other approaches, and never give up.

Acknowledgments

I am incredibly grateful for the educators who reviewed an earlier version of this book and offered valuable advice and feedback. These teacher scholars including John Brandt, Heather Brown, Ellen Condict, D. G. Hart, Caroline Hummel, Jack Hummel, Tabitha Loy, Jerilyn Olson, Maegan Satcher, and Jake Tawney.

I am also grateful for the fall 2021 pedagogy and apprenticeship students who used a draft of this text in class. These include Jaime Boerema, Mary Lou Brown, Anna Cannon, Aidan Cyrus, Anna Gjerde, Penny Heipel, Michayla Henes, Elizabeth Hughes, Sarah Johnson, Cate Kelley, Kathryn Luke, Paul Marselus, Matt McGrory, Matthias Rhein, Nick Schaffield, Isabella Sheehan, Brandt Siegfried, Natalie Stepanenko, Shelby Tone, Sydney Tone, Stephen Whitney, and Sonya Wilkins. I can't wait to see what amazing teachers you will become.

This little book began as a series of lectures for Hillsdale College's Barney Charter School Initiative. Without the support from the good people who work in Hillsdale's K-12 Office, this book would never have seen the light of day. I want to thank Kathleen O'Toole, George King, Eric Coykendall, Becky Lincoln, Jordan Adams, Tomek Grzesiak, Przemyslaw Grzesiak, Amelia Lawson, Nicholis Wagner, Kyla Engel, Ethan Greb, Julie Apel, Ethan Lehman, and Johanna Hunsbedt. I am grateful to have such talented colleagues and friends.

Hillsdale College Press could not have been better to work with. I would like to thank Doug Jeffrey, Tim Caspar, Matt Bell, Shanna Cote, Zane Miller, and Samantha Strayer. Their professionalism and dedication to their work only served to make this book better.

Most of all, I thank my beloved wife Kari for her steadfast support and unending encouragement.

About the Author

Daniel B. Coupland is professor of education and chairman of the Education Department at Hillsdale College and the dean of Hillsdale's master of arts program in classical education. He formerly served as the College's dean of faculty.

Dr. Coupland earned a B.A. in Spanish from Liberty University, an M.A. in linguistics from Oakland University, and a Ph.D. in education from Michigan State University. He began his career in education as a high school teacher. He has been at Hillsdale College since 2006 and teaches courses on English grammar, classical pedagogy, and classic children's literature. In 2020, Hillsdale College released an online course for the public based on his popular classic children's literature course.

Dr. Coupland has received Hillsdale College's "Professor of the Year" award and was awarded the Emily Daugherty Award for Teaching Excellence. He was a resident scholar at the C. S. Lewis Study Centre in Oxford, England, and he served as the editor for the *Journal for the Society for Classical Learning*. Currently, he sits on the advisory board for the Institute for Classical Education. His research focuses on general pedagogy, classic children's literature, and English grammar instruction.

Dr. Coupland has written for a variety for publications including *Academic Questions, Virtue, National Review, The Detroit News,* and *The Journal of the Society for Classical Learning.* He is co-author of an English grammar curriculum titled *Well-Ordered Language: The Curious Child's Guide to Grammar.* He and his wife Kari live in Jonesville, Michigan, with their three children: Quinn, Raegan, and Riley.

Appendices

Ten Books on Teaching
that Every Teacher Should Read

(Listed in Chronological Order)

1. *The Seven Laws of Teaching* (1886) by John Milton Gregory

2. *Goodbye, Mr. Chips* (1934) by James Hilton

3. *The Art of Teaching* (1950) by Gilbert Highet

4. *The Miracle Worker* (1956) by William Gibson

5. *The Paideia Program: An Educational Syllabus* (1984) by Mortimer J. Adler

6. *Begin Here: The Forgotten Conditions of Teaching and Learning* (1991) by Jacques Barzun

7. *The Elements of Teaching* (1997/2017) by James M. Banner, Jr. and Harold C. Cannon

8. *Why Don't Students Like School?: A Cognitive Scientist Answers Questions About How the Mind Works and What It Means in the Classroom* (2009) by Daniel T. Willingham

9. *Small Teaching* (2016) by James M. Lang

10. *Teach Like a Champion 3.0: 63 Techniques that Put Students on the Path to College* (2021) by Doug Lemov

Ten Effective Teaching Techniques that Every Teacher Should Use in the Classroom

(Listed in Alphabetical Order)

Activity	Description
1. Checking	Check students' understanding regularly. Ask a variety of questions, monitor students' nonverbal clues (e.g., facial expressions), give low-stakes pop quizzes, etc. Adapt and modify the lesson based on the feedback from these "checks."
2. Chunking	Combine related ideas, concepts, and facts into meaningful and manageable "chunks" (three to five items) and teach those chunks. Use graphic organizers and concepts maps to show these relationships. Our minds naturally look for these kinds of relationships, so use chunking to help students learn.

3. Dual Coding	As often as possible, use both words (verbal description) and images (visual representations) of the material to be learned. In other words, show *and* tell. Most students—regardless of their so-called "learning style" or preference—benefit from dual coding.
4. Interleaving	Have students focus on something intensively, leave it, work on something else, and then return to the original work. Interleaving encourages students to approach their work with fresh eyes and renewed vigor.
5. Moving	Move around the room while teaching. Teachers can teach from almost anywhere in the classroom. Not only does moving around make class more interesting for students, it also allows teachers to monitor and manage students' work and behavior better. Don't get stuck at the front of the room.
6. Predicting	Ask students to predict what will happen. Predicting activates students' prior knowledge, gives them an opportunity to invest in the topic at hand, and prepares their minds to learn.

7. Retrieving	Activate students' prior knowledge by reviewing previously learned material (from yesterday, last week, previous unit, last year, etc.). Ask students to put information and ideas into their own words. Retrieving is one of the most powerful—but underused—teaching techniques. Review, review, review.
8. Self-Explaining	Ask students to say out loud what they are thinking. Ask them questions such as: Why did you choose to do that? How did you come to that conclusion? What steps did you follow to get where you are? Teachers should also model their own "think alouds" for students.
9. Spacing	Cramming can be effective for short-term success, but it rarely leads to long-term learning. Break up activities (or practice), and have students do the work over an extended period of time.
10. Waiting	Don't lead a question with a student's name (e.g., "Lucy, why did the…?) because everyone not named *Lucy* will tune out. Rather, pose the question, *wait*, ask for an answer (volunteer or victim), *wait again*, respond to the student's answer or ask another student to respond to the original answer.

Ten Common Classroom Tasks that Most Likely Require a Procedure Because They Will Save You Time and Help You to Avoid Chaos

(Listed in Order of Importance)

1. Emergency drills (fire, tornado, active threat)

2. Restroom requests

3. Securing the students' undivided attention during class

4. Class dismissal

5. Students labeling materials correctly

6. Collecting materials from students

7. Distributing materials to students

8. Entering the classroom before the start of class

9. What students should do when they finish work early

10. Replacing a dull, broken, or empty writing utensil